West Coast, North Hill

Jan Petersen
Chris Culshaw
Trevor Matthews

007

This edition published in Great Britain by Flaxbooks,
26 Sun Street, Lancaster, LA1 1EW. Tel: 01524 62166.
www.litfest.org

Flaxbooks is the publishing imprint of Litfest
Lancaster and District Festival Ltd trading as Litfest
Registered in England
Company Number: 1494221
Charity Number: 510670

Editor: Sarah Hymas
Design and layout: Martin Chester at Litfest
Photography: Jonathan Bean

Acknowledgements

Jan Petersen's 'Coffee to Go' – published in *Coffee & Chocolate*, Leaf
Books 1977.

'Carolyn' (from 'Lake Trilogy') published in *Poetry Nottingham*.

ISBN
978-0-9558204-1-0

Contents

Biographies

Jan Petersen was born in Bristol to a family of Scots. She left school with one O Level and no game plan. After working in a variety of places, from a psychiatric hospital in Stoke-on-Trent to a record company in Los Angeles, she decided to get an education. In the mid 90s she returned to the UK and completed a first degree in Women's Studies and an MA in Writing Studies. Her poetry has appeared in magazines and anthologies, and her first play for radio was highly commended in a 2006 Radio 4 competition.

Chris Culshaw was born in Carlisle in 1943. He left home at 18 to work at Pilkington's glass factory in St Helens, before training as a maths and physics teacher. He taught in Liverpool for five years, before coming north to work at Morecambe High School as Special Educational Needs coordinator where he remained for over 20 years. Since retiring from classroom teaching in 1997, he has published over 150 titles for use in schools, and also worked as a tutor in Lancaster Castle Prison, Lancaster, and in mental health promotion.

Trevor Matthews spent his early childhood, during the Second World War, in rural Wales. In 1967, then a paediatrician working at Great Ormond Street Children's Hospital, he was seconded for two years to the University of East Africa, in Kampala, Uganda, at the time of the civil war. Other tours to the tropics followed. In 1972 he moved his home to the north-west. He still spent time overseas. Now, retired and living in the low fells, he has time to write about the people who live around him, and to reflect on the things in his life that he finds moving or important.

Foreword

The poems you are about to meet portray internal and external landscapes of three very different people living in the North West of England. As with any area, borders are not easily defined, we might be in one place, thinking of another, we might be about to leave, or have just returned. So these poems also travel across continents.

And because poems themselves blur boundaries – of poet, subject and reader – I hope you'll go willingly where they lead: into and out of yourself.

When this collection came together, I relished travelling its meandering roads. The people and stories in here feel as though they have been brought together by friends, family, friends of family, and a family of friends. Askance images of the seemingly innocent, a delight in speech and dialect, and the twist of honesty, all vie for position as the most memorable element of the volume.

What also struck me was the authenticity of the voices of these poets, the calm imperative with which they speak, and the illumination they bring to their subjects. These histories have become a part of my own history now, by my reading them. And I am enriched because of it.

These poems also stand many re-readings. Each time, they reveal more unexpected images and associations. Links and connections echo and bind the poems, so this collection grows beyond the individual poets. It is the difference that is the glue.

It has been a delight to bring Jan Petersen, Trevor Matthews and Chris Culshaw together in one volume. I hope they will open readers to a new imagined life, the gaps and unspoken thoughts that swirl around the streets, ghylls and people of this region.

Sarah Hymas

Jan Petersen

Bluegrass and Bluebells

The pope is dead. On the radio they're talking about his legacy. I'm driving and thinking of my father who left me twelve hundred pounds, two banjo mandolins I cannot play and memories;

of exploding bottles of ginger beer; the falling down wreck of a doll's house he tried to blame on Father Christmas; jaunts in his beloved Morris Oxford singing 'Loch Lomond' and sliding on leather seats when he took the bends too fast.

As a special treat he'd take me along when The Tumbleweeds played at the Miners' Club, Dad on banjo picked Flatt & Scruggs and Bert Cooper sang cowboy songs. After the break he'd take up his fiddle and they'd switch to the old Scottish tunes.

With tears and tantrums mother got her way, my dad left the band and everything changed. He said raising girls was a woman's job and gave me over to her spite. He still played his banjo but down in the shed so she couldn't complain of a headache brought on by the noise.

I moved to America where once I met Earl Scruggs' son. When I came back for good Dad was dying from forty years' dust on his lungs. For my guitar-playing daughter, hands blue-scarred and thickened picked a few bars of 'You are my Flower'.

The last time I saw him, he said *Make peace with your mother, it's a terrible thing to go with regrets.* And that's why I'm driving to visit a woman who will leave me with nothing at all.

Jan Petersen

New research proves it's good for you

I flash back to cold school mornings, dressing under the covers – vest, navy knickers, grey wool socks darned to rub. Dashing downstairs to claim the lumpy chair in front of a struggling coal fire. Tuesdays are best. Between *Bunty's* pages I can be a ballerina or a princess switched at birth. Not the child of this woman whose lips twitch with pleasure as she watches me gag trying to swallow my daily dose of foul fish oil.

Mother

The night before I gave birth I dreamed of her with me two weeks too long in her belly, a breech that couldn't be turned, legs forced apart, pain, piss, blood, male hands inside her dragging me out and was afraid I couldn't love my child if it was born with her face.

Jan Petersen

Outing

You take your children to the graveyard. Set out a picnic; banana sandwiches and lemon squash on the lichen top of a high tomb. They throw gravel at angels, dangle from an ancient yew, climb a Celtic cross encircled by nettles. Where the grass grows wild in remnants of ancient meadows, you seek out old stones. In a corner tented by shadows you twist wreaths of ivy, dog's mercury and belladonna. Trace the names of children who died young.

Dóttir

She's spending a year in Iceland, a country I know nothing about. We exchange emails. She tells me the population has just reached 300,000, the light is magical, people smile at her and roads are diverted to placate elves. She loves Reykjavik – it's cosmopolitan but cosy, sends photos of tin houses painted red and yellow and, because it's named after Hallgrimur Pétursson, a church that looks like a lava mountain. She's found a great place for pizza, always orders Kryddari. I like the word and make it my screen name. Outside the city she swims in the murky turquoise waters of the Blue Lagoon, drives through stark grey treeless landscapes brightened by flashes of colour from children's sweaters. For my birthday she sends a book of photographs – images in black and white, text in so-foreign Icelandic. At Christmas I hear of the Jólasveinar and the Yule cat that eats children who don't have new clothes. New Year brings the Northern Lights more spectacular than the Vancouver fireworks we once watched from a boat in English Bay. In the long dark winter she writes daily. Our relationship shifts into friendship. She's fallen in love. We talk about men and I confess I never chose wisely. *Does that include my dad?* She asks but doesn't get upset when I say *Afraid so*, and laughs when I talk about our wedding; the chapel between nail bar and liquor store in an Orange County strip mall.

Jan Petersen

Generation Gap

This is not my body. I weigh 110 pounds and this is more like 145, the skin is too loose and my clothes don't fit it. I don't know how to get the inside out and put the outside in so that's not all they see. What can I tell them so they know I've been young, quirky and cool, with the right look, music and friends, climbed Kilimanjaro in the wrong shoes, had sex in weird places, partied in Mexico and ate the worm? I saw Hendrix, Marley, the Boss, the King and have a photo in a drawer of me and the Colonel (not the one that fried chicken), had a live-in lover who played with Bowie – but that's name-dropping bullshit and my daughter's friend says her parents are sad because they listen to Dire Straits.

Last night I watched a retro film on women activists. I surfed the second wave on sex, drugs and rock 'n' roll, maybe that's how I washed up here beached and waiting for the Big Kahuna and hoping for redemption because I'm in the wrong body in the wrong place with the wrong people and I'm probably even the wrong mother for my so-right child. I'm not even sure this is my mind because I've been analysed, hypnotized, re-birthed, reiki-ed and rolfed and I am in control of my life.

A rabbi on the radio said The Messiah will come and breach the generation gap but she's not here yet and I need to talk this through. So I call my friend J. D., a molecular biologist with a passion for karaoke, who would leave the lab if she could sing, but she likes my anguish, says it's creative. So I wait for the right time to call Don in Palm Springs who has a Grammy in his loo. And when I'm done talking he says *Thank you for sharing*, and hangs up the phone. I laugh, pour a glass of wine and play 'Sultans of Swing'.

An Ocean Between Us

Sign on at midnight. Reality shifts as we move to a private room, a space safe for romance. I've learned to be mistress of artifice but feel a compulsion to expose bare bones while he slips on a silky screen persona. We play by his rules. I read between the lines. He lures me in. Words fly fast from my disembodied lover leaving me breathless. A pixellated image from another zone, he will never cross that sea.

 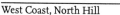

Jan Petersen

In Milt's Voodoo Lounge

Ray went down to Lincoln and Third for a couple of beers and to listen to The Dead played loud. He stood at the bar and watched a fat man in a damp shirt try to get close to the sad young girl who smoked French cigarettes. A woman with hennaed hair put a coin in the jukebox and smiled at Ray who said *I'm too old to dance.* (But too young to die). He took her hand. Redhead and Deadhead danced up a storm. That was before Milt got the karaoke. *Hey man, you gotta move with the times* he called as Ray walked away from the Voodoo Lounge.

Overheard on the Central Line

Nice leather. Saddle soap will soften it up. Shoe care's a thing of the past. I had a polish franchise for Natal and the Transvaal. Cheap Chinese footwear put paid to that. After my bypass the savings ran out. All the jobs were going to the Blacks. The wife has a post with a top car rental firm. I'll find something soon. This is your stop, *ja*? Take care of those shoes; they won't rub so much if you slow down.

 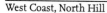

Jan Petersen

Closing Time

On the headlands above Fort Cronkite the sun warms my face, raptors circle above; down on Rodeo Beach black-bodied seals and surfers ride the waves. White pelicans fly in formation – a small boy, bright as a peacock, scrambling from bunker to bunker stops and aims his imaginary gun.

Yesterday I went back to Tiburon; our house is painted blue with yellow trim. Octoberfest was in full swing – you would have loved the band playing oom-pah-pah and mariachi. I ate a burrito down by the water looked across to Sausalito where we met in the bar with no name. Tomorrow there's a bluegrass festival in the park – you would have loved that too. I won't go.

Fog rolls across the bay, shrouding the bridge. *Before 9/11 you could stand right under it,* I tell the woman pointing her camera in that direction.

Jan Petersen

Los Angeles 1979

I got there too late. There was no spare sand.
Curves had straightened into lines. The city had an edge.

 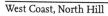

Jan Petersen

The First Time

A bottle of wine, the lure of the moon. They would have lain in a bed of nettles, but it was beneath the pier; rotting planks, corroded struts, dead seafood and litter of drift trash.

Jan Petersen

Coffee to Go

In line at the Starbucks on Robson I recognize a voice. When we hug I feel a familiar fire. His cell rings; he takes the call. I pick up my order. *Don't go*, he mouths. As I sip my tall cappuccino I see the manicure, $500 shoes, the crease in his jeans and know he still obsessively cuts his toenails. Still talking, he collects his venti double, non-fat, half-caf, vanilla latté, hold the foam, to go. I walk away. Again.

Jan Petersen

Promise of Spring

We walk past lavender and honeysuckle, pots of rosemary, parsley, thyme; out into the woods beyond the wall. You name the trees, point out the witches' butter on the birch, share the best spots to find wood blewits. In your grandmother's orchard you ask me to stay, promise come spring we'll smell the caterpillars.

I walk past patchouli and musk, coriander, basil, mint tied in bunches. If you were here I would name my favourite restaurants, point out the best store for shitake and black winter mushrooms. Why did you think I would want to smell caterpillars?

Lake Trilogy

i. Carolyn

I find the key under the pot you bought in Crete that cracked the day of Erica's wedding. A calico cat lies on top of bleached postcards, yellowed newsprint, curled coupons, drafts of poems abandoned when you became happy. Dust has settled on the books you loved but hadn't read in twenty years.

In the closet I run fingers over cotton tops – same style in different colours – your posh dress, the leather jacket you had forever, trying to absorb something of you through the stale tobacco.

From the window beneath the eaves where the wasps nested that last summer, the one that doesn't close, I can see the walnut tree and the lawn chair, rusty now, where you'd sit and watch dragonflies, electric blue, hover above the pond. And the rock garden Robbie made for you, hauling stones from somewhere along the Similkameen.

At the party (it wasn't a wake) the marquee on the lawn echoed with your laughter, throaty from the cigarettes that killed you off. We said *farewell* on a sailboat on Okanagan Lake and drank champagne as the wind took your ashes.

ii. Erica

The day her divorce came through Erica got a tattoo behind her ear. Along for the ride, I came out with a dragonfly. In Salty's beside the lake, we sit outside despite the autumn chill. A sulky waitress turns on the propane heater. The last plane to Vancouver flies low across the water, we watch the sun go down, drink Caesars and order up garlic prawns.

I read her my poem about Carolyn. Ripples appear on the smooth black surface of the lake. *Ogopogo* we say together. But there is no monster. As we get the check she asks *Do you think Mom knows I'm OK?* And turns her back to the wind to light a cigarette.

iii. Me

I drive past naked vineyards, fading signs offering tours and tastings, up to the house on Three Mile Road. The shutters are down, the key gone from under the pot; Erica's in Mexico – maybe she'll stay – we've said our goodbyes. I sit in the lawn chair. Breathe in the air. Someone's burning cedar. Carolyn's leather jacket keeps out the cold.

Across the lake SUVs head for the mountains. They'll be back next summer, hauling outboards and jetskis that churn up the lake. Today it is mine – deep, dark, obsidian-skinned. Calls my name from beyond the silence. I should get back in the car, drive to the airport, get on the plane to London. Quail scatter as I run towards the shore.

The Pretender

When Josh was two we rented a house on Stinson Beach, watched skim surfers, became rich with sand dollars. Afraid of the waves Josh sat in a bucket. When he was asleep we made love, broiled lobsters, drank Zinfandel and sang along to Jackson Browne.

You disappeared the third night in. A note in a bottle – *gone clear!* Ten years on I've stopped wondering why, but our son looks at photographs, sees your camera smile and blames me.

Jan Petersen

Survival

She speaks of women raped by dogs and kicked to death by soldiers on the streets. About that time I read 'Cosmopolitan' and strived for the perfect orgasm between designer sheets. She cried for her husband, one of the disappeared. Safe in suburbia, I would have gladly given mine. She could barely feed her child; my freezer was stocked with organic baby food. Her defiant words read aloud in secret places, gave strength. Mine blurred on contact with the pages of a silk-covered journal. She asks if I know the song by Sting, tells me his words were wrong. She danced La Cueca Sola in a sea of dancing women, never alone. Behind closed curtains, glass in hand, I swayed to Leonard Cohen.

Funeral Tea

You don't know what it was like in our house. You saw what she wanted you to see – whiter than white washing, donkey-stoned step, the flash of her outside smile as she placed half a crown in a newborn's hand. We lived with taunts, slaps, pinches. *I hear your whispers.* If I had just one happy memory I would have laid on a good spread with ham salad, cakes and perhaps even sherry.

Jan Petersen

Lost

You recall fragments. It's always summer. Creamy puffballs and sweet green grass; chasing katydids; leafwing butterflies; a cornfield, hot earth searing through thin shorts. A chair on a porch, whippoorwills calling from the trees, fireflies in a jar on a bedside table. I think it sounds straight out of a Faulkner novel. *Maybe it is*, you say.

Away Day

On a blue open-topped bus Lola met Robbie Williams. They started to talk. She missed her stop. He rolled down his sock so she could view his most recent and favourite tattoo. They got off at the pier where Robbie donned shades so he could fade into the crowd and have fun at the fair. On the Millennium ride he sang a few hits. Lola felt sick. So they took a walk, looked in shops, tried silly hats, bought sticks of rock. At the end of the prom in a posh hotel he ordered tea, cream cakes as well. She poured. He talked of the pressures of fame, poetry, love, Port Vale's last game. When the pot ran dry he said *Goodbye I'm off to a gig in LA.*

 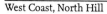

Jan Petersen

St Joan in a Penthouse

I won't light the candles. The moon, almost full, lights up the rooftops where tall chimneys are picked out in shades of grey. Below there are brighter lights but too far down for comfort. I peer out from behind velvet curtains, searching for a glint of moonlight reflected in his eyes or a movement in the shadows. I cannot see him but know he is there sending waves of malevolence across the chasms of the night. For a week he has waited with infinite patience, gathering strength to bridge the gap between buildings. I would be flattered if his motive was desire. I am cold. This is my sixth night without sleep. On the seventh day God rested, I will too. Tonight my devil will reveal himself – I saw it in the bones. I am ready. Courage swells my veins. I throw back the curtains. Here he comes, leaping across the black divide, crashing through the glass. My fingers tighten, surge with power. He's still. Blood, ketchup red, seeps from a round hole, surprisingly small, in his forehead. His mouth gapes. Laughter erupts from mine. Pounding on the door and voices. I turn in that direction and watch my hand with a will of its own fire the gun again and again and again.

Chris Culshaw

Chris Culshaw

One for Sorrow

Magpie on the Sky dish
pokes black holes
in my soap bubbles.

Chris Culshaw

Coming Clean

A bath is a lie,
soft soap's brisk frisk.
Purely cosmetic.

To come clean
we must sweat.
A bath is a lie.

The Cubist's Teapot

Its innards a mirrored maze, every twist
and turn clogged with decaying leaves.

It heaves up clots of tea, stains yet another
snowy cloth, slops every unsuspecting lap.

Chris Culshaw

Breakfast with Salvador Dalí

The toast, leathery as pterodactyl wings,
flapped and fouled the chrome-crumbed cage.

The marmalade, all charm and gold fillings,
groped the butter's monumental thighs.

When I asked for low-fat milk, the ends
of that malicious moustache twitched:
scorpions squaring up to mate or kill.

Sloth Fall

The butterfly overdosed on nectar,
flew blind through the forest night,
into the ear of a sleeping sloth.

The toe-claws uncurled, the sloth fell,
windmilling in slow motion, onto the
botanist's tent, sent the gas stove
bowling under the four-by-four.

The blaze of wild fire, caught in every
waking eye, like the stars brought
suddenly down to earth. Chaos slips its leash.

 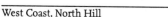

Chris Culshaw

The Rest

Food came on four feet,
poured through the valley,
fell into the pits, stoned to blood,
butchered. Plenty.

When the herds dwindled,
the fittest fed, the rest perished.
Dogs fought over their bones too.

When the herds stopped and could not
be found, the rest might have known
why, but they were just dust on the wind.

If God had had a Mother

No one on hand to wipe his snotty nose,
to tie the wayward lace, to teach him
the right from the wrong.

A gifted, headstrong boy who filled
his time magicking toys from nothing:
a star, a horse, a tree, you, me –
all culled from a fretful loneliness.

 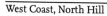

Chris Culshaw

Blue Baby

The tiny, wronged heart toiled. Lost,
until the scalpel made its mark.

Sudden hope fills our sails, as the
blood races beneath our daughter's bow.

Newborn Triplets

One day old, already an eternal triangle.
Six hands to hold. Not enough nipples.

Sardined under glass, an abacus of toes.
Nearly a little octopus. Ancient. Aquatic.

From this pale marbled flesh
each will carve their own likeness.

They taste the air and as they sleep
reach for hammers and chisels.

Chris Culshaw

Fathers and Sons

My father's great war was never won.
The sickness we called the Somme,
an iron nail in my father's heart.
He's long gone, but the battle's still not won.
The waste runs to rust in my blood and my son's.

The Eldest Son

When the purple velvet curtains still
and piped music stops, he is taken through
that door marked 'Private,' down a passage –
no carpets here – to a second (metal) door,
as heavy as a safe. Beyond, the furnace.

A brush against the wall nearby; Tippexed
on the handle: 'Dave's brush. Keep off.'

He is told to press the red button,
'Just once. No, harder.'
                              No sound,
as if what ever mechanism was activated
was far off, on another continent.

Chris Culshaw

Seafaring

Landfall, the pride and whisky
spent. I have come, at last, to settle.

The bow butts the bleached quay,
my bags swung ashore, engines idle.

Someone in a red beret waves.
The engines cough and storm away.

At the far end of the jetty, a brush,
its handle blackened with sweat
leans against a pram. The child
fast asleep, is seafaring.

Chris Culshaw

Horizon

My father's gone, cut down at a stroke. Now
an incomer will reap the crops he sowed last spring.

One last look. I walk Strand Meadow and the Dyke.
The sun a bleeding target. The horizon taut as a bowstring.

 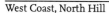

Chris Culshaw

Anatomy Lesson

First, understand your anatomy.

The ribs are, in fact, a cage.
The heart, in truth, a big cat.

Check all locks daily.

First Kiss

Fifty years on, and still alarming.

Under the canopy of dripping birches,
by the canal goose-pimpled with rain,
I learned that to be kissed is not the same
as kissing; that love's life's umbrella.

 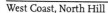

Chris Culshaw

Infatuation

Starts at the fingertips, prises open
the capillaries, homes in on the heart,
like fans converging on the stadium
for the final.

                         Too late for reason.
Turnstiles rattle like machine guns,
the arena waits; floodlit, manicured.

Yes, yes it's only chemistry,
idle chatter of nerve to nerve.
But that's no consolation. Here
in the hot glare of love, other rules apply.

Chris Culshaw

Unlikely Couple

New moon, old tricks.
Soft touch, hard kicks.

Sweet talk, sour rumour.
Light head, heavy humour.

Hot hands, cold shoulder.
First lie, last orders.

Chris Culshaw

Love Song

She was right. He was wrong.
She sang the words. He hummed along.

She told the truth. He told her lies.
She sang by heart. He improvised.

Chris Culshaw

There was an Old Woman

There was an old woman
who lived in a shoe:
slingback sneaker, electric blue.

Had seventeen children.
Knew just what to do...

 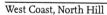

Chris Culshaw

Brackets

Desperate not to be bracketed with
the wrong Andrew, Claire Sumner scrawled
on the chippy's whitewashed gable end:
'I love Andrew (Wilson)'.

Outside the chippy, the wrong Andrew
talks about his latest bit of high-tech kit,
tries to ignore the girls' megaphoned
taunts about his spots, his pencil dick.

Andrew Wilson (the right Andrew),
eats his fill of everybody else's chips, wipes
his fingers on the wrong Andrew's parka.

West Coast, North Hill

Chris Culshaw

Shell

When you left, you made me
a present of the sea.

I hold the salted shell to my ear,
feel the rush of that parting kiss.

Chris Culshaw

Cartography

She is making a map of the known
world, scale one-to-one. Billions of sheets,
each the size of a bedspread.

'Put me on your map,' I beg. She laughs,
says, 'You move.' 'Rivers move. Mountains too.'
'That's true,' she says, 'But I like things fixed.'

I find a hammer and three six-inch nails,
take a sheet from the bed, lie, arms outstretched,
feet neatly crossed and say, 'Fix me.'

Chris Culshaw

The Gap

He lives in a bedsit now,
in a house peopled by footfalls, piles
of junk mail on the mahogany hallstand
where a broken umbrella hangs
like a snared crow beside the pocked mirror.

His room in the eaves looks out over
sooty privets, to a gap between
slabs of flats, where the river slides by,
and cranes shunt and stack containers
like draughts; night and day.

On certain days in late November,
the sun sets in this gap;
an ingot of honeyed light on his attic wall.
Queer, quiet moments, when he finds himself lost
somewhere between forgiveness and revenge.

Chris Culshaw

Back from the Gulf

The son did something very brave,
over there. Must have. Or why the medals?

Sleeps under his bed, dressed to kill.
His pillow a pile of dog-eared comics.

Dad wakes to find him kneeling, bayonet fixed,
boot-blacked face, outside the bathroom door.

An Iraqi boy without a face, watches from
the white-tiled foxhole, a father's awkward embrace.

Making Good

The Accused did it, no doubt about that.
He tore the child, confessed, cried out his life.
Gave himself over to some sort of god. Wanting
to make good. It was all written down.

The final meal, a Thai takeaway, extra rice.
Then he rolled up his sleeve, flexed
his muscles, made the tattooed heart stutter.
His last words: 'There. Put the needle there.'

 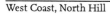

Chris Culshaw

Refuge

A blunt nub of pencil hangs on a string
by the payphone in the butt-strewn porch.

A boy plays cat's cradle, watches his father's face
through the wired glass in the steel-lined door.

His mother rips a page from the phone book,
snatches the pencil, scrawls 'No,' underlines it
seven times. Holds the paper to the glass.

The father's face again. Telly with the sound
turned down. The door shudders under
fists and feet. Boy and mother retreat.

The father's rage spent.
The pencil pendulums,
slows,
stops.

Chris Culshaw

Muhammad Ali at Sixty

His seconds wear starched whites
alive with static, smell of lavender.

They mop his brow between rounds,
slake his thirst, dole out dopamine.

The bruised blood thick with memory;
nerve ends pop and fizz like flash bulbs.

The famous fists fidget and ghost,
shadow-box with butterflies.

Chris Culshaw

One Night with Marilyn Monroe

My teenage wish turned flesh, suddenly
there she was, in my room, on my bed.
Said she just wanted to talk, tell me a bedtime
story about a girl in cast-off clothes,
waiting in line for stale bread, twenty-five cents
a sack. An orphan – and both mom and dad alive
and kicking. Passed like a parcel around
downtown Los Angeles where the old man
whose hands smelled of chicken fat
pulled her knickers down. Then the stammering
started and the beatings.

Not what I'd wished for, to be cried to sleep.

Divorce

She leaves his shoes outside, overnight.
The custom hereabouts.

Sensing the coming monsoon, the scorpion
chooses the right shoe, waits as still as Buddha.

Chris Culshaw

'Chickens'

Malik is fifteen – too old now – but
brother Oska, nine last Christmas,
he'll do. At midnight Malik takes
him to the railway station, leaves him
by the Coke machine, with the other chickens.

Next morning, six thirty, a young
policeman in a threadbare office
takes two dolls from the filing cabinet.
Unbuttons their gaudy clothes, shows
Oska the sewn-on genitalia.

Oska must tell his story; how the man
in the pale blue suit did 'this' then 'that.'
He asks about the trainers. The policeman,
wants to break the rules, but can't. 'Sorry,
we need them. You know: evidence.'

The Sin-Eater

I spread the starched napkin on the coffin,
asked, 'What kind of man was he?'
The undertaker whispered, 'You'll see' and
placed the steaming silver salver on the lid.

On a bed of watercress and chicory,
a small child, bound hand and foot,
eyes blinded by figs, her mouth an orange O.
'Ah, that kind of man,' I said, 'More mustard, please.'

 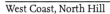

Chris Culshaw

Mother's Face Powder

Don't read into this any of that mother-son stuff,
no pseudo-Freudian parlour games, please. Don't
spray your uncertainties around like cheap scent,
tell me you never felt that urge to root through
the folds of silk and lace, never once
tried the lipstick or the powder, never once
stood before the mirror shaking, wondering what next,
what was brewing under that perfumed dust.

Trying

Have I tried? Of course I've fucking tried.
Six fucking years I've done nothing but try.
I've lost three fucking stone since she started.
What do you think I've been doing?
Fucking aerobics? Oh I've tried. We've all tried.

I've told her, that shit she puts in her arm,
I've told her. She's fucking me, fucking her kids.
It's like a war zone most days. Try and get near
her and you get tangled up in barbed bloody wire.

She'll do for me, she will. You can catch cancer
from stress, can't you? No, I don't want counselling.
Or family fucking therapy. Or what ever the latest thing is.
Just give me some fucking wire-cutters.

 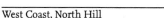

Chris Culshaw

After the Bomb

The baby was nearly a cousin. So
Kelly & Sons got the business.
The boss took me aside, asked:

'Are you up to it?' Said he'd show me how.
'The proper way to carry a kiddy. Right
arm under the head, left over the feet.'

Did a dummy run. Filled a wee bag
with fine sand. The white lacquered
casket more a cake than a coffin.

'No hearse, though. We'll use
the new limo. Put the casket
on the back seat. You ride up front.'

On the day I wanted that familiar
dead weight biting into my shoulder,
Mr K's arm locked over mine;

wanted to look down, see
black polished shoes,
measured, metronomic tread .

Neck and shoulders aching.
The tiny box stuffed with
something more dense than lead.

Trevor Matthews

Curiosity

The shelf held so many files, some of them labelled
Finance, or Gardening, or Income Tax
but the one that made me smile
was just called 'Interesting Things'.

Afterwards I opened it, and there were
cuttings from newspapers, pictures,
little objects, stones, dried seed cases,
pages from guidebooks and obituaries,

things he would have looked into,
examined again, given the time;
at the end I found one, the black ink fresh,
the last and lightest box of all,

that read, 'Still More Interesting Things'.

Trevor Matthews

Throwing Sticks for the Dog

The path had been rimed with frost all day,
the earth so bony hard it bruised the feet.
The stick I threw cut the whirling wind
like scissor shredding paper.

Where it struck the river,
spray rose in the sunlight,
hung in the air beneath the trees,
made a rainbow of refracted colour.

The dog, whining for release,
arched as an otter, leapt, swam,
snorted in ecstasy, seized the stick
carried it head high to the bank.

And then he shook his coat.
Spray flew wild about him
framed him in purple, yellow,
suddenly he was Resurrection Dog.

Later, trotting by my side, hair damp and sleek,
he stayed immortal. His energy
unmeasurable. My hand on His collar
and me feeding off Him, like a dynamo.

Snigging Timber

Charlie is scratching his head.
He has walked in the woods for an hour,
measuring alternatives with long
loping strides of his crane-fly legs.

The trees are o'er close to get at.
There's no room for t'Unimog,
but the hoss'll do the job all right.
Not as quick mind, and it'll cost.

He is relishing the moment.
I make it all the sweeter for him.
Will the horse be able to cope Charlie?
They aren't small, those trees I want taken.

He bridles, like I knew he would.
Cope? I'll say she will,
tha' doesn't knaw what a horse can pull
till tha's seen her at it.

Next day he brings a Dales pony,
her backside muscled like a wrestler.
Sweet long face, big lashes, rolling eyes,
fretting at the rusty chains she trails.

Charlie is away into the woods with her.
We hear the frantic chatter of his saw,
a tearing, shrieking noise, all birds silenced.
Then next the rattle of chains, a cracking,

and the pony strains through the trees
eight feet of log behind, soil churning,
brashed branch ends scraping a ragged furrow.

Na then, says Charlie with a grin,
That's not far off three quarter ton, downhill.
and pony herself is no'but half a ton...

This is the old alliance. Charlie waits quietly,
lean as a sapling, chin grey with stubble,
the pony grazing now, sweat steaming off her.

When they're dead there'll be no way to snig timber
except by tractor. Men will widen the gaps
between the trees, and the forest will leak out
and fade among the insubstantial fields.

Stoat

A grey afternoon,
February, and the light already going.
Outside my window a dry stone wall
is sieving the wind.
But still the casements rattle,
the only sound in this solitary room.
Ash slips through the bars of the fire
like snow.

The lichen on the sheltering wall take on,
in spring, the yellow flesh of pineapple,
then turn the green of Caribbean seas.
Today they're grey against the beckstone,
flat as gum on pavements, monochrome.
I push my chair back. Four oak feet
squeal on the flagged floor's surface,

and one of the stones moves, a quick
pivot of a small round head.
Poised on the wall, brown and still,
a stoat waits. The noise I make alerts us both,
me to his presence, him to my nearness.
His little shift sets free a feral scent.
The creatures that live in the wall smell him,
panic, scatter, sacrifice each other.

Briefly the stoat remains a statue,
a ruff of ermine at his neck.
He pauses for the choir of voles to clear,
then flows like water down the wall,
taking his measured bite first from one,
next from another,
arches into the long grass in pursuit of a third,
returns with blood on his breath.

Skies fade, darkness rises
from the frozen ground.
I draw the curtain on the scene,
wonder what the play should be called,
and whether to applaud.

My Neighbour Tells Me

there's more to lambing than lambs.
There's waking, red-eyed, finding
the old ewe's overlaid the good 'un,
dead as rags. The runt, where bye,
is snuffling at her tits, still not sucking.
Work there, for you, for someone.

There's more to lambing than lambs.
A sheep's not so clever. Weight of wool
can tumble her. On her back she's useless,
kesent, lies patient, waiting for crows
to peck at her eyes.

Sheep's very prone to dying.
Out there in the bracken,
never a bleat for help, silent,
hung up or tippled in a ditch.

You might as well have seen your bed.
Ugly beggars, coat hanging off them,
stained black and ragged,
muck soil for blowfly's eggs.

But then there's mornings also when the grass
shines like pencils. The crook
catches a small hoof, holds a lamb
and it's cradled in your arms
warm, clean smelling, black eyes
questioning, and you say to yourself
This is life, and I have it here
tight to my chest. My arm around it
and I can give it, safe, to the mother.

At that time I am shepherd of the sheep.
For that small moment.

Trevor Matthews

Counting Sheep

In Sussex us normally has two eyes,
know what I mean?
So us counts sheep in twos.
Why not? 'Tis twice as quick.
Here, watch this.
See that one there, the Suffolk by the gate,
the dog'll turn un and the rest follow.

G'wan away, go on.

Here her comes now, and one following.
Wuntherum.
And two more, close pressed.
Twotherum.
And a pause while the others gather
and clot like cream, a hard lump.
Watch 'em go round,
the old ewes together and the lambs
trying to break in to the circle.
Now here's the young ones coming
Cockerum.
Cutherum.
Shetherum.

That's ten through,
all your fingers used up,
now we mun start again.
I always like the second ten.
Toe sheep, I call them.
When you have your boots off
you'll see, words seem to go wi' feet.
The older ones is next.
Shatherum.
Wineberry.
Wigtail.

Where do they words come from?
Don't ask me. Go ask in the churchyard
'twas them there said 'em first.
Tarrydiddle.
Den.

Ten pairs there, twenty head, now start again.
Go on lad, your turn,
dog's still fetching.
Remember, wuntherum, twotherum, cockerum.
You'm not the first to have to learn these things.

Trevor Matthews

The Loaned Land

Just a rough paddock with a measure of dockings,
but somewhere all the same to keep the tups.
You're not using it? said Harold, *are you sure?*

That bleak shabby man, short, sweaty,
old coat torn and heavy with dirt,
growing more like his sheep each day.

Still, he cared for them, scythed the field,
came every night to rub their ears,
begged windfall apples for a treat.

One morning they were gone. *I've sold them*
he said, a finger at his nose,
Silly buggers, them was never any good.

Did you get a decent price?
Aye, not bad. But what's it count?
No one to need it, now that Mary's gone.

He scratched around a bit, picking up binder twine,
and the blue thing kept for drinking water,
so crudely cut from an old plastic barrel

that he must have used a chainsaw.
He threw it in the back of the pickup,
and nodded, *I'll be saying goodbye.*

I watched him drive slowly down the lane.
He needed watching. I didn't turn away,
never cared to with that mood on him.

And that was the last ever I saw him.
Without the tups he had no cause to be anywhere.
The inquest said 'an accident, a misread label.'

Well, he'd been walling for the coroner, hadn't he?
He'd had no sons, no daughters neither.
There was no one much at the funeral.

The paddock's still empty, and I noticed today
the dockings are coming back.

Trevor Matthews

Musing on High Things

A bishop, I learned today,
is always buried facing west,
so that he confronts his flock.

A nice conceit –
that even in death the bishop
thinks I am looking up to him. Instead

I have been watching,
through the candle's curling smoke,
the Third Duke's marble feet cast wavering shadows,

hearing the choir's last spare note
drift with the lightness of summer rain
against the worn risers of the chancel steps.

Round pillars sprout fine threads of stone,
high fragile webs above my disbelief.
Who were they built this church

those long-gone masons, worn hands
now neatly feathered into dust, none left
of flesh and sinew, muscle, nerve and brain?

I fancy for my Lords the bishops,
however high they place themselves,
things may prove just the same.

Ringing Shearwaters

We wrapped up, wool and heavy fleece.
A quiet night, but the wind
carried the edge of the sea with it.
It seemed colder in the dark,
what with the anticipation
and the standing around, rubbing hands
like making fire.
Underfoot the going was rough.
We needed the torchlight
to know where our feet were, and not
to trample the earthbound birds.
They lay bolstered by their burrows,
beaks stabbing in protest, bodies
awkward, attempting a rolling staggering
caricature of escape. So we let the warden
do the ringing, enjoying the gift of blackness,
the hiss of the waves and the seals calling,
the centuries old sounds of night-time
that will be there now, though we have gone
and our memories swim away from us.

 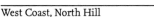

Trevor Matthews

The Mourning Tree

I have put three dogs underground this year
and Spring not yet finished.

They are safe in the field's curve, beneath a tree
I planted once, a sapling full of leaf,
then had to bucket water, day after burning day,
a slog each way through that summer of surprises.

She has grown high, this Arazonica,
downy and svelte, dense-canopied –
an ash who holds her buds furled, tight.
Spends but a brief time in leaf.

With the first frost she will drop her canopy
as a girl may do, stepping free
of mourning clothes. Leaving them
in a scattered ring around her.

And I shall know where the dogs lie
by the black circle of leaves, an armband
on a school jacket, the wearer shunned
lest he embarrass us with his weeping.

Little Bleak Poem

Walking down Penny Street I saw my father

Long dead, walking beside me,

His reflection in the window, stride for stride

Copying mine. He had even dressed

To match me. Same clothes. Same trainers.

Too young for him. The only difference

Was in the face. For I was young

And he had lines, and little hair.

And he did not stand up straight.

Trevor Matthews

The Annual Gathering

Coming through the court,
the familiar buildings,
I see them clustered in the corner.
Old men, grey, conscious of their stoop,
trying to stand tall.

A coppice of them,
crooked trees I knew as saplings,
a rustle of autumn leaves, counting
under their breath the numbers,
the absences.

The circle opens as I join them,
closes around me like a mouth,
hands greet me with the touch of paper
so that I feel I am breathing the dust
and ash of yesterday's fire.

Spadework

I am sorry that these days
graves are dug by machines
and no man throws out dirt
from the depth, as a mole does,

comes up for light, and air,
straightens the shoulders,
a black dampness on his back,
re-grips the spade and thinks

'that's near enough, just one spit more,'
then hawks, and gobs into the earth,
smiling at his solitary joke, certain
that no one's ever thought of it before.

I believe the grave's less cold a place
for his having toiled there,
for the shedding of his sweat,
the earthy fingered soiling of his face.

 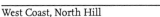

Trevor Matthews

Grasping Things

She was sitting at my kitchen table
looking at her hands.

These, she said, *are my mother's hands.*
She had big hands like these.
Every time I look at them now I see her,
and she held them up in front of me.

Bright sun pierced the thinning flesh.
Inside I saw the shadows of her bones
stand proud, like prisoners, waiting
on the margin of a common grave.

I looked at my own hands, and they were older –
knuckled and hardened.
I don't know, I said, *whose hands these are.*
I had an uncle who built boats.

My second son has thumbs like mine.
I have watched him planing wood,
the shavings curling softly at his feet
as if they were a loving dog.

We sat there, looking at our hands,
wondering if this might be flesh
our parents' parents once had used,
and this was what 'handing down' means?

Forestay

At times he would sail his small boat
and let the sea cause him to forget, until
the hour came to ease back into harbour
and anchor. Then he would stow the gear,
furl the two worn sails
that the wind had stretched,

go home to their granite cottage
and standing under the shower
let the salt spray sluice off him.
As the hot water spiralled down the drain
he would hum the tune of 'Lady Wrixton', or
'Give Me Your Hand', the 'Clergy's Lamentation.'

Later, washed clean of despair,
he would sit again by her lonely bed,
holding that other hand
whose fingers twitched
and tried to grasp at his
as he talked of tides and spray and wind,

while through the window, tossing at anchor,
he could still just see the outline of the headsail
tied up neat around the forestay,
the white spread of canvas bundled,
only the edge of it on show,
beneath the cover of the sacrificial luff.

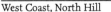

Trevor Matthews

Working Wood

Let the old blades show their worth.
File the jack's throat to take their bulk,
the heavy steel will stop the chatter.

Send the smoothing plane after the jack,
slivers as soft as a child's skin,
a curled carpet to quieten feet.

Ease the plane along the grain, raise
shavings so thin the light shines through them
as through hair brushed at a sunlit window.

Run a hand over the finished wood.
Feel where it rises and falls, small impressions
like lines on a weary face.

Now take sandpaper, cup it in your palm,
let your fingers choose where to press.
Remember when you held a wrist

then ran your hand slowly up another's arm,
lifting the fine hairs, the silent freckles
burning your fingertips?

Let it be like that. Press your lips
to the sweet smelling golden flesh.
You have found the heart of the tree.

Street People

They sit ignoring us, plucking a sometime chord,
when we drop a coin in their cap's sweated liner
we know no one will move a lip in acknowledgement.

And laying quiet on that same cold slab of street
their dogs are sleeping, always that odd gingery brown,
wrapped in tartan blankets, snoring,

waiting for polystyrene trays and curry scraps,
eyes closed beside some old campfire, or trotting
on red braided leads, when at last someone moves.

We are wary of them, the people,
but the dogs we can relate to.

Trevor Matthews

Self-build

Childless, you made the fabric of this house,
traced every salvage yard, sourced each beam,
tracked down mahogany, matched every stair,

telling me proudly, when we take the tour,
That window came from Marston Hall.
Look in Pevsner. You'll find it there.

I watch you stroke the golden fluted stone,
fingertips relishing the touch,
smoothing the mullions as if gentling hair.

Don't really want to quit you know, but
no one to leave it to, not getting younger,
so time perhaps for something simpler instead.

Hard to accept, I say, *yet very sensible.*
Garden's a problem when you're getting on.
You hesitate a while then nod your head.

I say goodbye, but as I go
you stand, there in the doorway
holding the handle like a small white hand.

Mending

You and our daughter, on your knees,
crouched over a cotton meadow, struggling
to tack in place the face and lining
of a patchwork quilt, the white wadding

trying to escape. Your backs wary,
rounded in concentration, there is
something of the gleaners about you,
a careful sweeping up of fallen grain.

I listen to the whispered murmurings,
the slide of scissors cutting cloth,
as above the workings of your hands
two voices stitch a reconciliation.

Trevor Matthews

The Boatman's Tale

They are, he said, looking towards the hills, *barbarians.*
They had their mortars up there, on the ridge,
and pouff, pouff, pouff they shelled this village.
What for? We are just fishermen, no soldiers here!
See the rooftops, the new tiles, the orange ones?
That's where the missiles fell. And that wall,
where the flowers are growing,
those are the marks of shrapnel. A girl died there.

He turned a fish over on the grill as if it were a corpse
and he was seeking its identity.

And now what happens? They are coming back
and the government pays them to rebuild their houses.
But not us. We get a few thousand German marks.
What can you do with that?
I tell you, he said, and his voice was loud
They are barbarians.

He turned the fish again, though it was not yet ready.

When a child is born we give the mother money.
They put a knife or a gun under the baby's pillow.
I became a commander in the army, and my brother,
he was eighteen years old, was killed a metre from me.
May they rot in hell. You go and visit them,
see what you think, next year,
then come back and we will have this talk again.

Below the boat fish moved like shadows,
not seen until one rolled
and, for a moment, let its underbelly flash.
First rule of camouflage. Stay still.

Friendly Fire

When he retired the General spent his time
deadheading the roses.
It was something to be done, no need
to bother with gloves or the best secateurs,
or the barrow, a cardboard box would serve.

Each year it had been the same.
He'd misjudge how many dead there were
and how the tiny infant thorns
would prick his fingers till he came away
with joints tingling, the job unfinished,

the faded blossom spilling and hanging
and always, though he tried hard to avoid it,
a few healthy roses captive in the tangle.
Such moments of carelessness,
misjudgements brought him brief regret.

And as he emptied the contents onto the bonfire
he said to himself there would be other rosebuds,
the bush would have a second flowering soon.
The loss of those few flowers would be seen
to justify the ends.

They always did, didn't they? In the long run?
People forget.

Trevor Matthews

Tranquillity

There is a man at the end of our road
who studies the stars. At night I see him
in his glass observatory, watching, watching.
The glint of brass from his telescope moves
as it follows the moon's shift.
In the daytime he wanders around his garden,
stares between the branches of the trees,
searches for the Sea of Tranquillity.

He talks to himself like a child who gives her dolls
names and tells them what they are to do.
He intends to order the planets to his command,
make them follow the arcs and circles
that he traces with his feet in the wet, dewy grass.
He hasn't yet worked out the finer details
but he thinks he is getting closer.

Before he was ill he was sure he knew about such things.
The treatment took away his sense of scale.
He feels now that if only his arm was that bit longer
he could reach upwards, outwards and capture the stars.
I have seen him stretching up towards them, groping
for the end of his telescope, fingers laced into a sieve.

In spring I found him weeping on a grassy bank,
torn stems and daffodil petals all around.
They were sending rays, he said, *through their trumpets,
so I broke them. You did right*, I said
and took his hand and led him back into his garden,
where the laburnum was in bloom,
the panicles of yellow blossom dropping
like that girl's hair in the tall, closed tower.

I took some fallen petals in my hand.
Let's use these to confuse them, I said,
and threw them up into the air
where they made a golden dusty haze.
There, it's ray-proof, nothing will get through that.
He looked at me, a long and puzzled look.
Some people do very strange things, he sighed
and walked away, closed the door to his house,
and from inside I heard a piano play
a plangent tune I should have recognised.

Trevor Matthews

September Harvest

What is it with God
that He had to make crane flies?
There He is, finishing the tortoise,
done the ostrich, the ring-tailed lemur,
when He peers into the bottom of the bag,
turns it upside down, shakes it,
and out drops a handful of insect legs,
a little body and a set of long thin wings.
He attaches the wings, sticks a few legs in,
turns the body over, shakes His head,
takes a few legs off again,
joins them onto the others.
They sort of pop together, like Lego
and suddenly the crane fly's there
standing up tall on its six long legs, looking worried.
He blows it off the palm of His hand
and it flies, all its wings whirring,
makes a circuit of the room, comes in to land.
Though it doesn't do that too well.
When he tries to help it up two legs don't work anymore.
But it's a game little thing, flies off pluckily
though only as far as the fine white curtains
where its remaining legs get tangled
in the mesh of cotton
and the more it struggles the more legs
fall off, or break, fragment,
turn to a grey smudgy dust
so that when God shakes the curtain
the crane fly falls onto the floor, looking dead.
He opens the door, meaning to swoosh it outside
but the night wind takes it
and with a flutter of its wings
it vibrates off into the warm wet air, towards
the long grass with the misting pollen
where it settles soft like spider's web.

And God looks at it go and thinks:
Well maybe it's not a great flyer
but it surely is a triumph of function over form
and after all the experts will say later
the bumblebee can't fly at all! And pauses.
But hold on, He says, *I am The Expert.*
At which point he smiles, fondly.

It had been a heavy week.

Trevor Matthews

My Empty Valentine

I wanted to buy you red roses
but a man on a quad bike
rode off with them all,
his arms full of cellophane and promises.
I've none left now said the woman,
and smiled smugly.
There's only the bucket.
How much for the bucket? I said.
10p, she joked.
I'll have it, I said, dropped
a coin on the counter
and quick as an eel
took it by its metal handle.
And three quid for the water, she called.
Don't need the water, I called back
and tipped it out on the dirty pavement
where it made a shape like Africa.

So I give you this bucket, very clean,
empty of everything but my love.
Yet shake it and it will rattle,
for my love is made of grass and pebbles,
soft bits and hard bits.
Giving and receiving love is like this bucket.
It could hold anything you choose.
Fill it too full and it will flow over
and be wasted. Let it hold just the right
amount and it will be easy to carry.
It is bright and shiny, and nothing
can tarnish it but time.

Drystone Wall

When I was a child I took to bed
a soft toy and a dictionary, went
hunting in the blanket dark of torchlight

for the big ambitious words
like igneous, ashlars, sarcens,
words that would signify stones,

heard them clack as they stacked
neatly, one on top of the other,
all in their different weights and colours.

Years on I still hold them ready, lest
I stumble on a gap that wants
their triple curves, their planes and angles,

needs them to partner all those others
that are lined up at the side.
It has been a long wait

and I am thinking
that they may never be used
and that certain gaps are not meant for mending.

I am laying these words
on paper, as a wall
built in an old man's way.